FIGHTER
interceptors

DATE DUE

BRODART, CO.   Cat. No. 23-221

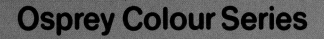

Osprey Colour Series

FIGHTER
interceptors

AMERICA'S COLD WAR DEFENDERS

René J Francillon, Peter B Lewis and Jim Dunn

Acknowledgement

Additional photographs are reproduced by courtesy of Jean-Pierre Bézard, Maj Gen Wayne Gatlin, Christian Jacquet, Lockheed Corporation, Douglas D Olson, Robert Pfannenschmitt, Carl E Porter, and Daniel Soulaine.

Published in 1989 by Osprey Publishing 59 Grosvenor Street, London W1X 9DA

British Library Cataloguing in Publication Data

Francillon, Rene J. (Rene Jacquet, 1937–
    Fighter interceptors: America's cold war defenders.
    1. American fighter aeroplanes, 1945–1987
    I. Title   II. Lewis, Peter B.   III. Dunn, Jim
    623.74'64'0973

ISBN 0-85045-932-X

Editor Dennis Baldry
Designed by Paul Kime
Printed in Hong Kong

Front cover F–101F–105–MC (58–0294) of the 179th Fighter Interceptor Squadron, 148th Fighter Interceptor Group, Minnesota Air National Guard over the colourful woods of Minnesota in the autumn of 1972 (*Courtesy Maj Gen Wayne C Gatlin, MN ANG*)

Back cover Wearing a distinctive black and blue stripe just forward of the intake, this F–106 belongs to the CO of the 318th FIS, based at McChord AFB in Washington

Title pages A beautiful Florida sky appears to challenge Montana's claim of being the 'BIG SKY COUNTRY' as a Convair F–106A–85–CO of the 186th Fighter Interceptor Squadron taxies at Tyndall AFB during the 1982 William Tell Weapons Meet

17th DEFENSE SYSTEMS EVALUATION SQUADRON

4756 AIR DEFENSE SQ. TYNDALL AFB FLORIDA

319th FTR INTCP TNG SQ USAF INTERCEPTOR WEAPONS SCHOOL

95TH FTR. INTCP. TNG. SQ.

Introduction

In 1945, immediately after VJ Day, the Army Air Forces deactivated the last early warning radar stations in the US, and the nine-month old Continental Air Forces were quickly brought to a virtually dormant status. Thus, upon being activated on 27 March 1946 to organize and administer the integrated air defense system of the Continental US . . ., exercise direct control of all active measures, and coordinate all passive means of air defense,' the AAF Air Defense Command had little to administer, exercise, or coordinate and was without teeth. It assumed control of the 414th Night Fighter Squadron, a purely paper organization, and the 425th NFS, manned by one officer and two enlisted men. The Cold War, in particular the Soviet blockade of Berlin in June 1948, and the explosion in the Soviet Union of a nuclear device in August 1949 and a thermonuclear device four years later, quickly changed all that.

By the mid 1950s, ADC reached its peak strength of 69 Fighter Interceptor Squadrons (with North American skies also being guarded by 68 Fighter Interceptor Squadrons of the Air National Guard, two All-Weather Fighter Squadrons of the US Navy, and nine CF-100 squadrons of the Royal Canadian Air Force). Since then, however, the threat of manned bombers has decreased and with it ADC strength has been allowed to dwindle. Thus, at the beginning of 1988, dedicated air defence forces in the United States were back down to six active squadrons (the 48th, 57th, and 318th FIS and the 1st, 2nd, and 95th TFTS) and 13 Air National Guard squadrons (the 114th TFTS and the 101st, 111th, 119th, 123rd, 134th, 136th, 159th, 171st, 178th, 179th, 186th, and 194th Fighter Interceptor Squadrons).

Notwithstanding these opening paragraphs, this book in no way seeks to pass for a history of air defence forces in the United States or of the aircraft used in that role. It is merely a collection of photographs of some of the NORAD aircraft and units from the late 1960s to the present. We only sought to share with aviation enthusiasts, and particularly our younger friends who will never have a chance to see and hear a pair of Century-series interceptors bolting on alert, Kodachrome memories of a colourful period.

As we did in a previous title in the Osprey Colour Series, we ask you to forgive us if in the midst of these 120 photographs you do not find one of your favourite aircraft or squadrons. We argued at length which slides to include and which to leave out. In the end, we decided to include along with Deuces, Voodoos, and Delta Darts, the airborne early warning and 'friendly enemy' aircraft without which interceptor pilots could not have accomplished their missions or trained realistically. Hopefully, our selection will help fill gaps in the collection of our younger friends and the bright splashes of colours on the following pages will bring back happy memories among those who shared with us a most interesting period in aviation history.

René J Francillon, Peter B Lewis and Jim Dunn
Vallejo, California, January 1989

Right Lt Col Richard M Stultz, a 43-year old pilot with the Flight Test Branch of the Sacramento Air Logistics Center at McClellan AFB, is assisted into the cockpit of 57–2453 by a Chief Master Sergeant of the Montana Air National Guard on the occasion of the completion of the last major overhaul of an F–106A in January 1986. Col Stultz flew 3280 hours in F–106s. first with the 456th FIS at Castle AFB and then successively with the 11th FIS at the Duluth International Airport, the 87th FIS at KI Sawyer AFB, the 48th FIS at Langley AFB, and the Sacramento ALC. He was also involved with the Delta Dart during tours of duty at HQ NORAD and HQ ADTAC

Contents

Out of Sixes, Out of Fighters

Standing forlorn in a downpour during the summer of 1967, this F-106A bears the Hat-in-the-Ring markings of a noted Air Force squadron, the 94th. As the 94th Pursuit Squadron, the unit gained fame flying Spad XIIIs during the last eight months of World War 1. As a Figher Interceptor Squadron, the 94th flew F-80Bs between December 1948 and March 1949. It then was transferred to SAC before returning to ADC in April 1950. The 94th FIS flew F-106s from Selfridge AFB, Michigan, beginning in April 1960 but was deactivated shortly after moving to Wurtsmith AFB, Michigan, in December 1969. In 1971, it was activated once again as the 94th TFS (*Courtesy Douglas D Olson*)

Above In its second existence as an interceptor unit, the 71st FIS changed bases no fewer than six times. Transferred from the Strategic Air Command to the Air Defense Command in April 1950, the 71st moved three months later from March AFB to George AFB, both in California. It moved twice more during that year, to Griffiss AFB, New York, in August and to the Greater Pittsburgh Airport in October. The squadron remained in Pennsylvania until going to Selfridge AFB, Michigan, in August 1955 and then to Richards-Gebaur AFB, Missouri, in January 1967. It settled at Malmstrom AFB in June 1968 and remained in Montana until its deactivation on 1 July 1971

Above Activated at Kinross AFB (later renamed Kincheloe AFB) in Michigan, the 438th FIS was successively equipped with F-94Bs, F-89Ds, and F-102As before converting to F-106s in May 1960. One month after this F-106A was photographed at Kincheloe AFB on 10 July 1968, the squadron moved to Griffiss AFB, New York. There it was almost immediately renumbered 49th FIS, the change becoming effective on 30 September

Left A Delta Dart from the 11th FIS caught in the alert barn at the Duluth International Airport, Minnesota, on 12 July 1968. Two and a half months later, the squadron was redesignated the 87th FIS

Above Briefly flying Republic F-47Ds after being activated as a Fighter Interceptor Squadron at Grenier AFB, New Hampshire, in November 1952, the 48th FIS moved to Langley AFB, Virginia, early in the following year. It has remained there ever since and flew Sixes from the autumn of 1960 until converting to its present F-15As in 1982

Left Previously equipped with F-102As and based at Suffolk County AFB, New York, the 5th FIS moved to Minot AFB in February 1960. One of its F-106As was photographed at this North Dakotan base on 17 July 1968. The 5th FIS remained at Minot until deactivated in 1987

Above Concurrent with its move from Richards-Gebaur AFB, Missouri, to Malmstrom AFB, Montana, in June 1968, the 71st FIS adopted more colourful tail markings

Above Caught in the late afternoon sun, a 159th FIS F-106A of the Florida ANG gently banks over McClellan AFB in California. The 159th usually calls Jacksonville International Airport home

Right An attractively marked F-106A of the 27th FIS at McClellan AFB, California, on 22 May 1971. The squadron was then based at Loring AFB, Maine, but two months later it was transferred from ADC to TAC with whom it became an F-4 squadron assigned to the 1st TFW at Langley AFB, Virginia

Above An F-106A of the 49th FIS taxiing past F-101Bs from the Maine and Oregon Air National Guard and F-106s of the 87th FIS and Montana ANG during William Tell '76. The 49th FIS, which was deactivated at Griffiss AFB on 1 July 1987, was the last active unit to fly the Delta Dart. The first F-106As had been delivered in May 1959 to the 498th FIS at Geiger Field, Washington, and to the 539th FIS at McGuire AFB, New Jersey. Other active duty Fighter Interceptor squadrons which flew Delta Darts were the 2nd, 5th, 11th, 27th, 48th, 71st, 83rd, 84th, 87th, 94th, 95th, 318th, 319th, 329th, 437th, 438th, 456th, and 460th

Right The 87th FIS, which had been renumbered from the 11th FIS at Duluth Airport in September 1968, moved from Minnesota to Michigan in May 1971 and remained at KI Sawyer AFB until deactivated in the mid 1980s. One of its F-106As is seen here landing at Tyndall AFB during William Tell '76

Above The 171st Tactical Reconnaissance Squadron of the Michigan Air National Guard was reorganized as the 171st FIS in July 1972. At that time it exchanged its McDonnell RF-101Cs for F-106As. One of its Delta Darts is seen here at McClellan AFB, California on 30 October 1977

Above The large clamshell canopy was a distinctive feature of the two-seat F-106B as shown here by an aircraft from the 101st FIS at Tyndall AFB on 23 September 1978. This Massachusetts ANG unit converted from North American F-100D Super Sabres to Delta Darts in 1972 and was redesignated 101st FIS in June of that year. For the next 16 years, until converting to its present F-15As and F-15Bs, the 101st FIS flew F-106As and F-106Bs from Otis ANGB

A pair of F-106As from the 48th FIS taking off at Tyndall AFB on 25 September 1978. Based at Langley AFB, Virginia, the 48th FIS has long pulled alert duty at the Florida base and is still doing so with its F-15As and F-15Bs

Opposite above This F-106A of the 84th FIS is landing at Castle AFB, California, on 19 April 1979 with its weapons bay doors open due to an inflight failure during a training sortie. An AIM-4 blue training round can be seen on the forward launch rails

Opposite below Framed against the backdrop of a desert range, this F-106A-105-CO of the 5th FIS lands at Nellis AFB, Nevada, on 26 January 1981 after taking part in a Red Flag training mission

Above An F-106B from the USAF Aerospace Defense Weapons Center taking off at Tyndall AFB on 26 October 1982. The gear has already retracted and the doors are closing as the aircraft accelerates at the start of a training sortie over the Gulf of Mexico

Left The Delta Dart was developed to meet the requirements for the 1954 Ultimate Interceptor as defined in an Advanced Development Objective released in January 1949. It was initially conceived as a development of the Delta Dagger and was tentatively designated F-102B. The design evolved considerably and justified the assignment of a new designation. As shown in this head-on view taken at Tyndall AFB on 22 October 1982, the F-106 was indeed considerably cleaner than the F-102

Above After a demonstration curtailed by poor visibility, Lt Col Richard Stultz taxies back to the ramp during the F-106 closing-out ceremony at the Sacramento Air Logistics Center on 18 January 1986. On that occasion, the mount of Col Stultz was a 27-year-old immaculately clean F-106A of the 186th FIS, Montana Air National Guard

Above 57-2453, an F-106A-65-CO of the Montana ANG, starting its 24,500 lb thrust J75-P-17 turbojet. The 186th FIS was the first Guard unit to transition to Delta Darts, doing so in April 1972. The five other Guard units which flew F-106s were the 101st FIS in Massachusetts, the 119th FIS in New Jersey, the 159th FIS in Florida, the 171st in Michigan, and the 194th FIS in California

Right The 119th FIS of the New Jersey ANG was the last Guard unit to fly F-106s, doing so until the spring of 1988 when it converted to F-16As. The bulges beneath the fuselage of 59-0031 and 59-0033 each house a 20 mm M61A1 Vulcan cannon

29

Red Surrogates

Two specialized Defense Systems Evaluation Squadrons, the 4713th DSES at Stewart AFB, New York, and the 4677th DSES at Hill AFB, Utah, were activated in 1959 by the Aerospace Defense Command to provide realistic simulated targets for its interceptors. Typical of the most numerous version of modified B-57s operated by these squadrons, 55-4280 is an EB-57E with ECM gear in the weapons bay and a chaff dispenser beneath each wing. Twin scoops beneath the J65 air inlet identified aircraft fitted with Sundstrand engine-driven AC generators providing power for the ECM equipment

Opposite above Photographed at Hill AFB on 3 July 1968, this B-57E of the 4677th DSES retains its SEA camouflage. It has not yet been modified to the EB-57E standards as evidenced, notably, by the absence of ECM aerials beneath the fuselage

Opposite below Bearing the badge of the Aerospace Defense Command on its fin, this RB-57D-0 of the 4677th DSES was built as a single-seat high-altitude reconnaissance aircraft with wing span increased from 64 ft to 106 ft. After serving with SAC units, a dozen RB-57Ds were operated by ADC in the defence evaluation role

Above An ex SAC RB-57D-2 of the 4677th DSES at Hill AFB on 3 July 1968. After being retired from covert operations following fatigue problems, RB-57Ds had their wings strengthened prior to being transferred to ADC for use as high-altitude aggressors

In 1974, the 4713th DSES was deactivated and the 4677th DSES, which by then had moved to Malmstrom AFB, Montana, was redesignated 17th DSES. An EB-57E from this unit is seen here on the transient ramp at Mather AFB, California, on 5 April 1975

Opposite above Based at Forbes AFB, the 117th DSES of the Kansas ANG flew EB-57s for just over four years between 1974 and 1978. A pair of its EB-57Bs visited McClellan AFB, California, on 17 September 1975. The black smudge on the forward portion of the engine nacelle was made by cartridges used to start the Wright J65-W-5 turbojets

Opposite below An aircraft of the 17th DSES in bicentennial markings at McClellan AFB on 18 September 1976. With no ECM aerials beneath its fuselage, 55-4238 is identified as a B-57E trainer

Above After flying F-51Ds, F-94As and Bs, F-89Ds, and F-102As, the 134th FIS became the 134th DSES in June 1974. Still attached to the ADC, this Vermont ANG unit then flew EB-57s until converting to F-4Ds during Fiscal Year 1982. Its bicentennial-marked EB-57B was photographed at Tyndall AFB during William Tell '76. The nose-down stance of the aircraft is noteworthy

Above Also seen during William Tell '76, this bicentennial EB-57E of the 17th DSES is the same aircraft shown on pages 30–31 in the markings it carried in 1968 while serving with the 4677th DSES at Hill AFB

Right An EB-57B from the 134th DSES landing at McClellan AFB in December 1980 displays ECM aerials beneath its fuselage. The nickname of the Vermont Guardsmen, *The Green Mountain Boys*, is painted on the outboard of the chaff dispensers

Opposite above First to complement and then to supplant its EB-57s, ADC made extensive use of T-33As. Although they could not carry some of the more powerful ECM gear fitted to the larger and more powerful EB-57s, the T-33As carrying chaff dispensers and/or ECM pods proved effective in the role of 'red surrogates'. This T-33A carried the markings of the 49th FIS when it was photographed at Tyndall AFB in October 1976

Opposite below A T-33A from the 159th FIS taxies from the Guard ramp at Jacksonville International Airport on 3 October 1978. At that time, the primary mission aircraft of this Florida ANG unit was the F-106A

Above Finished in an unusual scheme, this T-33A from the 48th FIS was photographed at Tyndall AFB on 21 October 1982. The squadron retained its T-33As after transitioning from F-106As to F-15As during that year

Above In addition to distributing T-33As among Fighter Interceptor squadrons, the Aerospace Defense Command, and later ADTAC (Air Defense Forces, Tactical Air Command), used T-33As as the sole equipment of Fighter Interceptor Training Squadrons. The 95th FITS at the USAF Air Defense Weapons Center was the last active unit to fly T-33As, doing so until re-equipped with F-15As and Bs in 1988. This T-33A from the 95th FITS carried an ECM pod beneath the port wing and a chaff dispenser beneath the starboard wing when it was photographed at Tyndall AFB on 21 October 1982

Right Three T-33As from the 84th FITS are in tight formation near the Fresno Air Terminal as their active duty pilots prepare to show their colleagues of the California ANG how a tactical break should be executed

Deuces and Starfighters

Not designed as an interceptor and lacking radar, the Starfighter was placed in service with the Aerospace Defense Command almost by default; Tactical Air Command no longer wanted the F-104 and ADC needed supersonic aircraft due to delays with the development of its F-101Bs and F-106As. This pair of F-104As from the 83rd Fighter Interceptor Squadron based at Hamilton AFB, California, is seen in 1958 flying over the Ferry Terminal Building and the western end of the San Francisco–Oakland Bay Bridge in San Francisco

Left After serving with ADC for less than three years beginning in December 1957, F-104As and Bs were transferred to the Air National Guard to equip the 151st FIS in Tennessee, the 157th FIS in South Carolina, and the 197th FIS in Arizona. In Guard service, the 104s deployed to Europe during the Berlin Crisis in 1962. They were then returned to ADC service with the 319th FIS at Homestead AFB, Florida, and the 331st at Webb AFB, Texas, when the Cuban Missile Crisis revealed the need to have fast climbing interceptors based opposite Cuba

Above The 82nd FIS at Travis AFB, California, transitioned from F-86Ds to F-102As in August 1957. Eight and a half years later, this squadron became the first to be equipped with F-102As modified for air refuelling and was thus able to deploy across the Pacific to assume air defence duty for Okinawa. Not yet modified, this F-102A from the 82nd FIS was photographed at Oxnard AFB, California, on 21 June 1964

Above Still bearing the ADC logo on its fin, this F-104B photographed at McClellan AFB, California, on 13 April 1968 last served with the 331st FIS at Webb AFB, Texas. This squadron had been deactivated on 1 March 1967 and most of its Starfighters were eventually transferred to the Royal Jordanian Air Force or converted as QF-104A drones

Opposite above F-102As from the 179th FIS on the Guard ramp at Duluth International Airport, Minnesota, on 12 July 1968. These Deuces had last served with active duty units in Alaska and thus retained high visibility Arctic markings

Opposite below A part-time Guardsman working for TWA has neatly 'zapped' this TF-102A from the 176th FIS, Wisconsin ANG, seen at Truax Field on 13 July 1968. The high drag of its side-by-side accommodation prevented the TF-102A from reaching supersonic speeds in level flight

The Deuce had a long and difficult gestation and was fitted with difficult-to-maintain avionics. Conversely, it was one of the safest Century series aircraft and was well liked by its pilots. Photographed at Hector Field on 15 July 1968, this F-102A belonged to the 178th FIS, North Dakota ANG. The 'Happy Hooligans' flew Deuces between July 1966 and November 1969

Left The 186th FIS, the only flying unit of the Montana ANG, converted from F-89Js to F-102As in July 1966 and was re-equipped with F-106As in April 1972. Still based at the Great Falls International Airport, where this F-102A was photographed on 17 July 1968, the 186th FIS now flies F-16As

Above A black-bordered yellow boomerang adorned the F-102As and TF-102As of the 153nd FIS. Based at the Tucson International Airport, this Arizona ANG unit flew Deuces from February 1966 until September 1969 when it became an F-100 replacement training unit

Opposite above Belonging to the 157th FIS, a South Carolina ANG unit based at McEntire ANGB in Columbia, this F-102A was photographed on the ramp of the California ANG at the Ontario International Airport on 20 March 1970

Opposite below After being released from active duty in July 1952, the flying unit of the Florida ANG was redesignated 159th FIS. Since then, it has been equipped with F-51Ds and Hs, F-80Cs, F-86Ds and Ls, F-102As and TF-102As (between the summer of 1960 and the autumn of 1974), F-106As and Bs, and F-16As and Bs

Above In addition to the 190th FIS illustrated by this March 1970 photograph and the previously mentioned 152nd, 157th, 159th, 176th, 178th, 179th, 186th, and 190th Fighter Interceptor Squadrons, Deuces equipped 15 more ANG squadrons, the 102nd in New York, 111th and 182nd in Texas, 116th in Washington, 118th in Connecticut, 122nd in Louisiana, 123rd in Oregon, 132nd in Maine, 134th in Vermont, 146th in Pennsylvania, 151st in Tennessee, 175th in South Dakota, 194th and 196th in California, and 199th in Hawaii

FREDDIE'S LADY, a TF-101F-110-
MC of the 18th FIS, was seen at
Grand Forks, South Dakota, on 15
July 1968. Having entered service
in January 1959 with the 60th FIS
at Otis AFB, Massachusetts, the
interceptor version of the Voodoo
was phased out from ADC service
in the spring of 1971. The 18th FIS
at Grand Forks, South Dakota, was
one of three squadrons deactivated
at that time

Voodoo Power

Below The 2nd FIS at Suffolk County AFB, New York, flew F-101Bs from August 1959 until deactivated in December 1969. The taped tail of one of its Voodoos, an F-101B-100-MC, was photographed in the boneyard at Davis-Monthan AFB on 17 March 1969

Bottom In July 1959, the 13th FIS left the Sioux City Municipal Airport in Iowa, from which it had been flying F-86Ds and F-86Ls since 1955, and moved to Glasgow AFB in Montana. There the squadron flew Voodoos, including this F-101B-90-MC, until its deactivation in June 1968

Still carrying the markings of the 49th FIS, a unit which had been deactivated 10 days earlier at Griffiss AFB, New York, this Voodoo was photographed at Grand Forks, South Dakota, on 15 July 1968, after it had been transferred to the 18th FIS

Above The infrared sensor forward of the windshield replaced the
retractable inflight refuelling probe initially fitted to Voodoo interceptors.
With its large clamshell canopy open, this TF-101F-96-MC of the 62nd FIS
at KI Sawyer AFB, Michigan, clearly shows the sun shield mounted over the
radar scope in the rear cockpit

Above Based at Lockbourne AFB, Ohio, the 87th FIS converted from F-102As to F-101Bs in June 1960. It was deactivated in July 1968, but its designation was almost immediately given to an F-106A unit at Duluth International Airport, the 11th FIS, in one of several ADC renumbering exercises (*Courtesy Douglas D Olson*)

Above Photographed at Travis AFB, California, on 25 August 1968, this F-101B-85-MC belonged to the 332nd FIS which flew Voodoos from Kingsley Field, Oregon, between April 1959 and September 1968

Opposite above Activated at Charleston AFB in February 1954, the 444th FIS was deactivated at this South Carolina base in September 1968. It flew F-86Ds until the spring of 1957, F-86Ls for the next three years, and Voodoos until its deactivation (*Courtesy Douglas D Olson*)

Opposite below This Voodoo of the 445th FIS at Wurtsmith AFB, Michigan, displays the characteristic rotating weapons pallet of the F-101B and F-101F and the twin-blade aerials for the SAGE (Semi-Automatic Ground Environment) data link system beneath the aft fuselage (*Courtesy Douglas D Olson*)

Above Photographed at Tyndall AFB on 25 September 1978, this Voodoo
of the 2nd FITS was fitted with an experimental sensor in a fairing beneath
the nose cone

Above The 116th FIS in Washington, the 132nd FIS in Maine, and the 178th FIS in North Dakota became the first Guard units to fly F-101Bs when they converted from F-102As in November 1969. This 'MAINEiacs' F-101B is seen taxiing at McClellan AFB, California, on 17 September 1973

The 'Happy Hooligan's from Hector Field flew Voodoos from November 1969 until March 1977. One of their TF-101B trainers basks in the late afternoon sun on 11 March 1973 after a typical Californian winter storm had turned parts of the Fresno Air Terminal into a lake. A camouflaged F-102A of the 194th FIS, California ANG, can be seen behind the Voodoo's nose

Above A Voodoo from the 123rd FIS, Oregon ANG, at Tyndall AFB during William Tell '76. That year the Oregonians won in the F-101 category, and one of their crews, Maj Bradford A Newell (pilot) and Lt Col Donald R Tonole (WSO), won overall Top Gun honours

Right Voodoos participated in ten William Tell competitions between 1961 and 1982. This 123rd FIS aircraft is seen on final approach to Tyndall AFB on 1 October 1978

The William Tell '78 winner in the F-101 category was the 111th FIS.
Based at Ellington AFB, this Texas ANG unit flew F-101Bs for ten years
beginning in May 1971

Warning Stars

Left To provide adequate warning of air attacks, the DEW (Distant Early Warning), Alaskan, Mid-Canada, and Pinetree radar networks were complemented in the 1950s by picket ships, sea-based radar platforms (the so-called Texas towers), and AEW aircraft. The 4701st AEW&C—the Air Force's first Airborne Early Warning and Control unit—was activated at McClellan AFB on 1 October 1953. This EC-121T was photographed at this Californian base on 25 September 1971

Below With flaps down but gear still retracted, this EC-121Q from the 552nd AEW Wing is seen here on the downwind leg prior to landing at McClellan AFB on 30 January 1973. In addition to its ADC operations on the east and west coasts of the United States as well as in Iceland, the wing was kept busy during the South-east Asian War by the need to provide Big Eye and College Eye Task Force detachments for operations in the war zone

Left While aviation enthusiasts bemoaned the Warning Star retirement, air and ground crews were less sentimental as poor engine reliability had led the former to experience many tense return flights over water and the latter to pile up much unwanted overtime. With cowling panels open, this EC-121Q provides a sombre reminder that Warning Stars, along with similarly-powered civilian Super Constellations and DC-7s, were nicknamed the 'World's best trimotors'

Above Even though dorsal and ventral radomes spoiled the beautiful silhouette of this Super Constellation derivative, the Warning Star remained a most attractive aircraft

Left After the war in South-east Asia ended, the need for war weary Warning Stars diminished greatly and the 552nd AEW was reduced from Wing to Group status in July 1974. Less than two years later, on 30 April 1976, the Group was deactivated at McClellan AFB

Above In addition to various models of the EC-121, the 552nd AEW Group operated a few TC-121Gs, including 54-4062 seen here at McClellan AFB on 4 March 1974, to train Warning Star flight crews

One of the last EC-121Ts of the 552nd AEW Wing on approach to McClellen AFB on 27 February 1975. Its starboard fin is adorned with the eagle emblem of the Aerospace Defense Command

Phantoms, Eagles and Falcons

Although many CONUS and Alaska-based Tactical Fighter Squadrons flew their F-4s in a secondary air defence role, the only active Fighter Interceptor Squadron to be equipped with Phantom IIs has been the Iceland-based 57th FIS. This squadron replaced its F-102As with F-4Cs in April 1973 and took five of these aircraft to Tyndall AFB for William Tell '76

Left In 1982, when the 57th FIS next participated in a William Tell Weapons Meet, its camouflaged F-4Cs had been replaced by grey F-4Es including this F-4E-32-MC (66-0336) and F-4E-35-MC (67-0315)

Above An F-4C from the Air Defense Weapons Center landing at Tyndall AFB on 1 October 1978

Above Carrying an AN/ALQ-119(V) ECM jammer pod beneath its port wing, this ADWC F-4C was playing the role of an aggressor for a Profile IV sortie (interception of aircraft using ECM) during William Tell '78

Right Whereas the F-4 saw little use as an interceptor while in service with active units, it became the most important interceptor of the Air National Guard. With the 194th FIS of the California ANG, F-4Ds replaced F-106As during the winter of 1983 and were retained until the end of 1988

Above The 171st FIS at Selfridge ANG first replaced its F-106As with F-4Cs during Fiscal Year 1978 but later exchanged them for F-4Ds. While equipped with F-4Cs, the 171st FIS took part in the 1982 William Tell Weapons Meet

Right While the 86th TFW was converting from F-4Es to F-16Cs in 1986, the alert duty normally assigned to this USAFE wing based at Ramstein AB was given to the Air National Guard with F-4Ds and crews from various Fighter Interceptor Squadrons being sent TDY (temporary duty) to Germany. Armed with live Sparrow and Sidewinder missiles, this F-4D from the 179th FIS, 148th FIG, Minnesota ANG, was photographed in front of the alert barn at Ramstein AB in June 1986

Left Flaps and slats down, an F-4D from the 178th FIS, North Dakota ANG, is caught over the threshold at Tyndall AFB on 1 October 1978. During the previous year, the 'Happy Hooligans' became the first Air Guardsmen to be assigned Phantom II interceptors

Above Bearing on its fin the name of the airport where it is based rather than the name of the state to which it belongs, this F-4C from the 136th FIS, New York ANG, is one of many MiG killers which ended with Guard units

This double MiG killer F-4C
63-7647 now serving with the
123rd FIS, awaits completion of
safety checks before taking off for a
training sortie from the Portland
International Airport on 8 July
1988

With its wings folded, this F-4D of the 111th FIS could not deny its naval ancestry when it was photographed at Ellington Field, in October 1987 (*Courtesy Daniel Soulaine*)

The most potent aircraft yet to be assigned to Fighter Interceptor Squadrons is the F-15A. However, only four F-15 operational squadrons have been assigned interception as their primary mission while three others have received Eagles to train interceptor pilots. The 48th FIS at Langley AFB, with a detachment standing alert at Tyndall AFB, was the first unit of F-15 interceptors and was to have been equipped with aircraft modified to launch the ASAT anti-satellite missile

Opposite above Just like their brethren from Tactical Fighter squadrons, F-15 pilots from Fighter Interceptor squadrons regularly deploy to Nevada to take part in Red Flag exercises. The 5th FIS at Minot AFB flew Eagles for only three years before being deactivated a few months after this F-15A was photographed landing at Nellis AFB in July 1987

Opposite below Fitted with conformal tanks, this Eagle landing at Nellis AFB on 7 October 1987 bears the markings of the 57th FIS, an Iceland-based TAC unit. The 57th FIS converted from F-4Es to F-15Cs during the summer of 1985

Above Due to become the last active duty Fighter Interceptor Squadron, with deactivation likely before the end of 1989, the 48th FIS has replaced its attractive air defence markings with the LY tailcode in keeping with TAC's more common style of markings. This F-15B, the flagship of the First Air Force, is seen here on the ramp at Tyndall AFB on 18 October 1988

Above Montanan F-16As from the 186th FIS in dubious company at the Reno-Cannon International Airport, Nevada, on 15 September 1988. The MiG-21 in the foreground and the MiG-15 in the background are aircraft imported by Aviation Classics Ltd. (earlier known as CIA, Classics in Aviation) at the Stead Airport near Reno

Left After converting from F-4s to F-16As in 1986, the flying unit of the Vermont ANG initially retained its Tactical Fighter Squadron designation. However, its primary mission and designation were changed two years later; the Green Mountain Boys were once again designated 134th FIS as they had been from 1951 to 1974 while flying F-51s, F-94s, F-89s, and F-102s

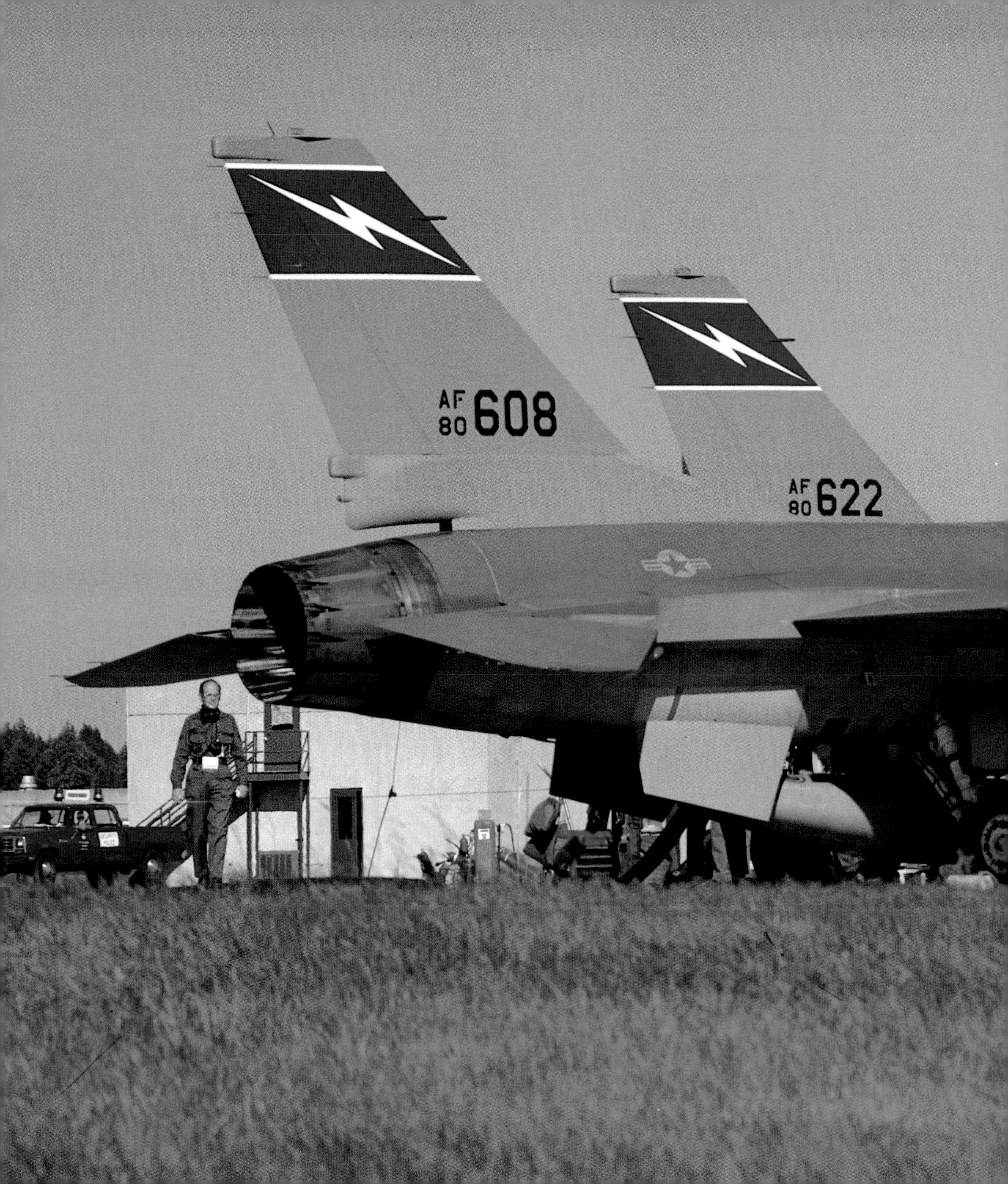
AF
80 608
AF
80 622

No such redesignation was necessary for the 159th FIS which converted from F-106As to F-16As during Fiscal Year 1988. Almost immediately, pilots from this Florida ANG unit began intercepting Soviet transport and maritime patrol aircraft straying into the ADIZ (Air Defense identification Zone) during flights to and from Cuba

Droning Away

Old fighters never die, they only drone away. . . . In addition to using drone versions of its obsolete fighters and bombers in support of missile testing programmes, the Air Force has increasingly used fighter drones as targets for its interceptors. This PQM-102 was photographed at the Air Defense Weapons Center in October 1976

PQM-102s were first used for William Tell in 1978. Thereafter red-tailed drones were seen at Tyndall AFB in a variety of colour schemes with some aircraft painted light grey while others were camouflaged

Above and opposite above Two views of 56-1223, an F-102A-65-CO modified as a PQM-102A by Sperry Corporation Flight Systems as part of the Pave Deuce program

Opposite below QF-100 drones were first used during a William Tell Weapons Meet in 1984 to provide realistic, highly manoeuvrable targets against which competitors could fire radar and infrared guided missiles. In addition, during ECM exercises, piloted QF-100s carry ECM pods such as that seen under the port wing of 56-3324 taxiing at Tyndall AFB on 21 October 1982

Above The trailing edge of a QF-100 damaged by an inert AIM-9 launched by 'Beaver 4', one of the 123rd FIS F-4Cs taking part in William Tell '86

Opposite above 56-3855, one of the three QF-100Fs assigned to the 82nd Tactical Aerial Targets Squadron, 475th Weapons Evaluation Group at Tyndall AFB in early 1988. At that time, the ADWC drone unit also had 58 QF-100Ds. Ten QF-100Ds and Fs were shot down during William Tell '88

Opposite below To complement and eventually replace its QF-100 drones, Tactical Air Command has begun to use QF-106 drones. An ex-87th FIS F-106B and an ex-ADWC F-106A modified as drones on the ramp at Tyndall AFB on 19 October 1988

Canadian Cousins

At the height of the Soviet bomber scare in the mid 1950s, the United States' first line of defence extended from Alaska to Greenland. Fortunately for the United States, Canada provided the vital link and contributed nine squadrons of Avro Canada CF-100 all-weather fighters stationed at Comox, British Columbia; Cold Lake, Alberta; North Bay and Uplands, Ontario; and Bagotville and St. Hubert, Quebec. After being replaced as interceptors by McDonnell CF-101s, a number of CF-100s were brought to Mk 5C and 5D standards and used by the Electronic Warfare Unit and No 414 Squadron as electronic aggressors. Prior to the phase-out of these aircraft in October 1981, several were painted in special commemorative schemes. This Mk 5D was photographed at Abbotsford in August 1981 bearing a scheme similar to that which had been applied to CF-100s serving with the No 1 Air Division in Europe

Opposite above Also seen at Abbotsford in August 1981 with Mt Baker in the background, this aircraft from No 414 Squadron had been repainted in a scheme recalling that of the first CF-100 prototype. Noteworthy features of the Mk 5D were the T aerials above and below the rear fuselage, the chaff pods beneath the wings, and the ECM cooling intake in place of the gun port of Mk 4 and Mk 5 interceptors

Opposite below In 1961–62, the Royal Canadian Air Force obtained 56 CF-101B interceptors and ten CF-101F operational trainers to replace CF-100s still equipping Nos 409, 410, 414, 416, and 425 squadrons. As part of Operation Peach Wings, these late production Voodoos were traded between 1969 and 1971 for upgraded F-101s being phased out from ADC service. Photographed at Davis-Monthan AFB on 10 May 1971, these two aircraft from No 416 Squadron were among the last Canadian aircraft involved in this exchange

Above A scary moment at McClellan AFB on 3 July 1973. The high heat of a central Californian summer day caused fuel in the overfilled tanks to expand and vent off over the exhausts, forcing this No 425 Squadron crew to abort take-off. The backseater anxiously leans out to look aft as the pilot of this CF-101B ponders whether to shut the engines and be pulled to the ramp or to taxi back on his own power

Left Hawk One Canada, serial 101012, the beautifully finished CF-101B displayed by No 409 Squadron at Abbotsford in August 1977

Above Based at Comox, British Columbia, No 409 (Nighthawk) Squadron flew CF-100s between November 1954 and early 1962 when it converted to CF-101Bs. Now equipped with Hornets, No 409 Squadron is based at Sollingen, West Germany, as part of the 1st Canadian Air Group. This pair of Canadian Voodoos was photographed at Abbotsford more than 19 years later

Above Marked Lark One Canada on the port side and Alouette Un Canada on the starboard side in keeping with the bilingual status of the Canadian Armed Forces/Forces Armées Canadiennes, 101014 from No 425 (Alouette) Squadron was photographed at London, Ontario, in June 1984 (*Courtesy Daniel Soulaine*)

Right An inflight engine fire forced the pilot of this CF-18A from No 410 (Cougar) Squadron to return to Hill AFB on 20 July 1988 and request that the arresting gear be rigged for an emergency landing. At touch down on Runway 14, the arresting hook created a spectacular display. All ended well for the Canadian pilot and his Hornet

Air Defence People and Weapons

A Delta Dart pilot goes through his cockpit checks while waiting to taxi out of the alert barn. His F-106A is fitted with the clear canopy which was retrofitted to improve visibility after Delta Dart pilots began being trained for air combat against enemy fighters in addition to retaining their primary mission as bomber interceptors

Opposite above Lt Col Glen P Doss, Commander of the 84th FIS, and his back-seater, await authorization to taxi from the transient ramp at McClellan AFB on 10 March 1981. A little over three months later, the 84th became a Fighter Interceptor Training squadron and traded its Delta Darts for T-33As. For Col Doss and the other pilots of the 84th, the proud saying 'when you're out of sixes, you're out of fighters' took on a particularly painful meaning

Opposite below Texans are fond of asking fellow Americans 'I'm from Texas, what country are you from?' Apparently pushing this Texan braggadocio a bit further, the pilot and WSO of an F-101B from the 111th FIS, Texas ANG, fly the Texas flag as they taxi back to the ramp at Tyndall AFB during William Tell '76

Above Major Loren English, in the cockpit of 52-1551, an EB-57B from the 134th DSES, prepares for departure from McClellan AFB at the start of a flight taking him back to the Vermont ANG base at the Burlington International Airport on 12 December 1980

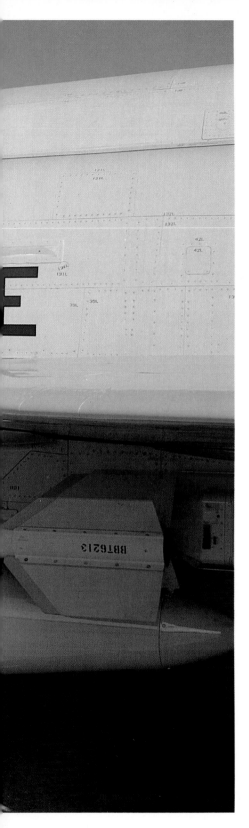

Left Like Tactical Fighter Squadrons, Fighter Interceptor Squadrons have in recent years relied on infrared guided Sidewinder missiles as one of the primary weapons carried by their aircraft. This AIM-9P is seen on the No 2 station of an F-4D from the 178th FIS, North Dakota ANG, at Tyndall AFB for William Tell '86

Above Except when on alert or on a few special occasions, F-4s based in the United States are seldom seen with a full load of Sparrows and Sidewinders as carried by 66-7485, an F-4D from the 136th FIS, New York ANG, at Niagara Falls on 17 September 1986 (*Courtesy Robert Pfannenschmitt*)

Green Dragons

Right The 318th has carried the Fighter Interceptor Squadron designation longer than any other unit. The squadron was based at McChord AFB, Washington, and equipped with Lockheed F-94As when it was redesignated on 1 May 1951 from 318th Fighter All-Weather Squadron to 318th FIS. It successively moved to Thule AFB, Greenland, in July 1953 and to Presque Isle AFB, Maine, in August 1954, prior to settling back at McChord AFB in August of the following year. The 318th FIS is expected to be deactivated during the summer or early autumn of 1989. Meanwhile, it is still maintaining its two-aircraft Detachment 1 on alert at Castle AFB, California, a duty it picked up in October 1981 after the 84th FIS had exchanged its F-106As for T-33As and had been redesignated the 84th FITS

Below The markings used by the 318th FIS during the early seventies are illustrated by this April 1972 view of the tail surfaces of a late production F-106A-135-CO

Above Revised markings were adopted by the squadron in the late seventies. The 318th FIS at McChord AFB converted from F-102s to F-106s in March 1960. Less than six years after this F-106A was photographed at McChord AFB on 4 August 1978, the 318th converted to F-15As

Opposite above Framed against Mt Rainier, this T-33A from the 318th FIS was photographed at the start of a training sortie from McChord AFB, Washington, on 2 June 1986

Opposite below Wheels and flaps have already been retracted as 76-0099 climbs in front of Mt Rainier at the start of a training sortie on 2 June 1986

Above An F-15A from Detachment 1 of the 318th Fighter Interceptor Squadron photographed from the back seat of a T-33A of the 84th Fighter Interceptor Training Squadron during a flight off the coast of central California on 18 September 1986

After the scheduled deactivation of the 318th FIS during the summer or early fall of 1989, its F-15As and F-15Bs are to be transferred to the 123rd FIS at the Portland International Airport to replace the old F-4Cs of this Oregon ANG unit. This Det 1 aircraft was photographed in the alert barn at Castle AFB on 25 January 1989. It was not yet known which unit, if any, would take over alert duty at Castle AFB after the deactivation of the 318th FIS